If You Can See The Dark

By Timothy Mudie and Jenny Ward • Illustrations by Mattie Rose Templeton

Appalachian Mountain Club Books
Boston, Massachusetts

If you can see the dark . . .

Fireflies can find their friends and moths can find their food.

Lights at night can be so bright that fireflies can't see other fireflies light up, and they can't find each other. Moths and many other bugs fly toward the bright light instead of searching for food. Have you seen bugs flying around outside lights?

If you can see the dark . . .

Bats can find their breakfast and bees can help us grow our own.

People wake up when the sun comes out; bats wake up when it goes down. If there are too many bright lights outside their home, bats think that it's daytime and don't come out to eat. When animals like bats, beetles, moths, and bees visit flowers, it helps to grow more flowers, including some of your favorite fruits and vegetables!

If you can see the dark . . .

Birds and butterflies can travel around the world.

Animals use moonlight and starlight to show them where to go at night. Bright lights distract them from the ponds and forests where they want to go.

If you can see the dark . . .

Little animals can sneak and hide.

Opossums, mice, and other animals need to hide-and-seek to find their food—and to make sure they don't become food themselves! When it's dark, it is easier for them to stay in shadows and keep other animals from seeing them. Many animals see even better at night than we do during the day!

If you can see the dark . . .

Birds and frogs know when to sing.

Birds sing in the day. When there's too much light that is not from the stars and moon, they might think it is daytime and not get enough sleep to be healthy. Frogs croak and peep at night to find their friends. If they think it's daytime, they might forget to sing!

If you can see the dark . . .

Fish can have happy lives.

Nighttime light affects fish and other aquatic life, too. It lures fish away from their hiding spots to where bigger fish can find them, and slows the growth of amphibians like frogs and newts. No one wants to stay a tadpole forever!

If you can see the dark . . .

Trees can grow and flowers can blossom.

Plants blossom in the spring and drop their leaves in the fall. When it is too bright at night, flowers can bloom too early and trees can drop their leaves too late. Would you want to wear a heavy coat and mittens in the summer?

If you can see the dark . . .

You can see the stars.

Thousands and thousands of them. And not only stars, but planets and even the white band of our galaxy, The Milky Way. Drawing lines that connect the stars makes pictures called "constellations." There are the Big Dipper and Little Dipper, Leo the Lion, Draco the Dragon, and many more. Imagine all the stories you could tell about them . . .

If you can see the dark . . .

You can sleep as soundly as a bear.

Everyone sleeps better when it's dark: a great big bear, a tiny chipmunk, or even you! Animals use darkness to know when it's time to go to bed and time to wake up. Getting a good night's sleep helps living things stay healthy and grow up big and strong.

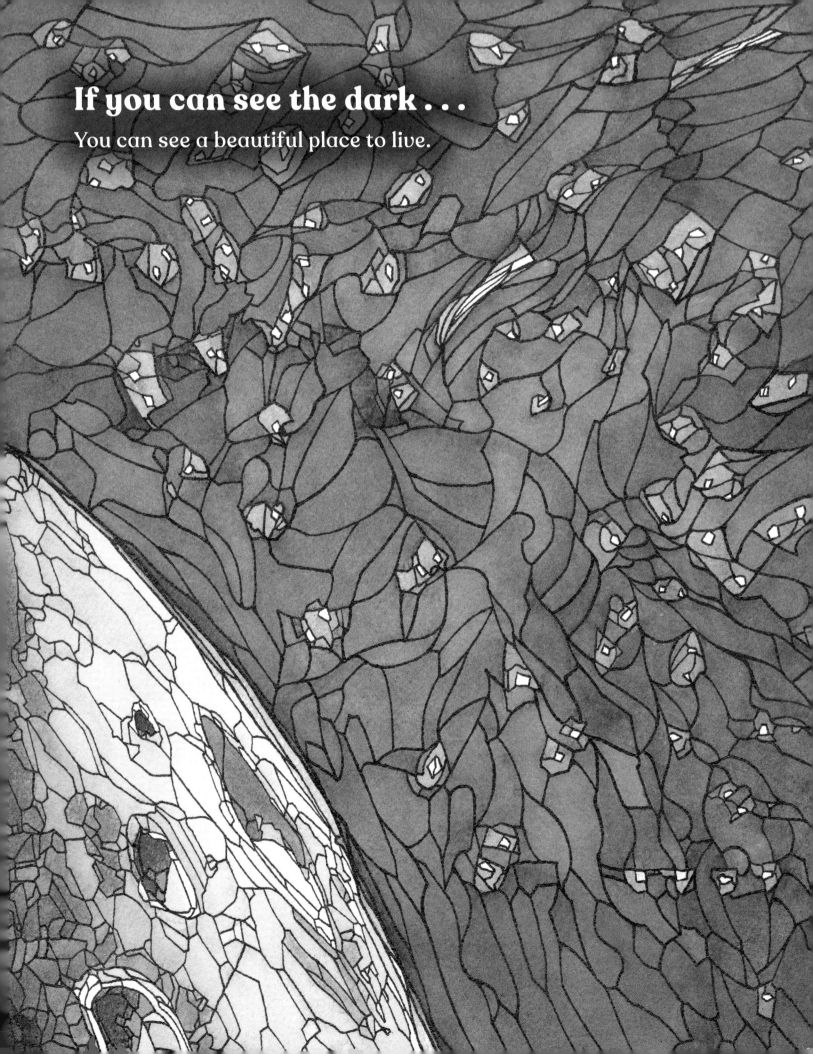

If you can see the dark . . .

You can see a beautiful place to live.

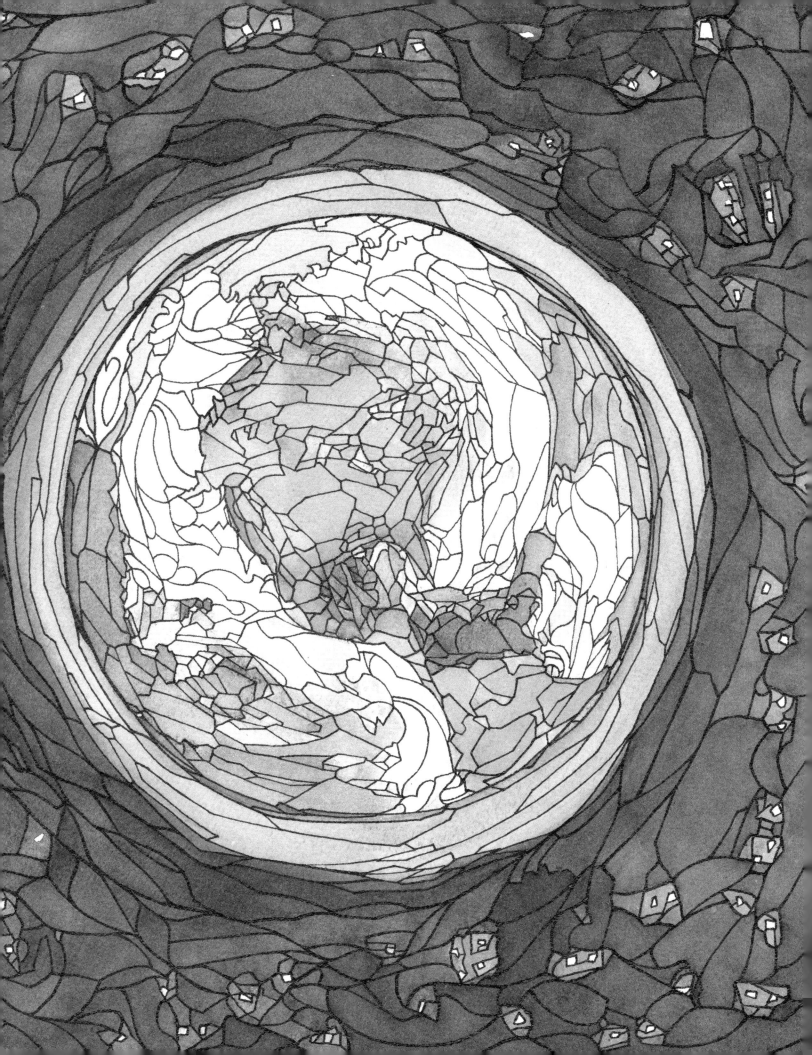

What is a Dark Sky?

A dark sky is one where artificial light does not interfere with the view of the natural starry environment. One hundred years ago, anyone could look up at the night sky and see thousands of stars above, but due to the increased and widespread use of artificial light over the last century, 80 percent of the world's population lives under skyglow, and in the United States and Europe, 99 percent of the public can't experience a natural night.

What are the benefits of dark sky conservation?

The conservation benefits of limiting excess artificial light include:

- Reducing deaths of migratory birds, turtles, and other species that interact with the natural night sky

- Improving wildlife habitat, including supporting natural pollination of plants and recovery of plant and tree species

- Reducing the pollution associated with energy production

- Immediately returning visibility of the stars in the night sky

There are broader benefits to reducing light pollution as well, including:

- Saving homeowners, municipalities, and businesses on energy costs

- Reducing glare, which improves street safety

- Providing science education and light pollution awareness through dark sky programming

- Opening the door to establish an astro-tourism economy in the region

How can you help?

- Talk to others about the benefits of dark skies and risks of light pollution

- Participate in community science—there are a number of ways to measure and share information related to dark skies

- Support good outdoor lighting policies in your town, rehab poor-quality outdoor lighting installations at your home or business, and reach out to educate neighbors and visitors on the importance of dark skies

- Sign up for alerts to AMC's calls to action at outdoors.org/CAN

- Donate, join, volunteer, advocate

Visit

The AMC Maine Woods International Dark Sky Park lies at the edge of the North Maine Woods, an expanse of more than 14,000 square kilometers of largely uninhabited forest land that stretches from Monson, Maine, to the border of Canada. This region is one of the darkest places remaining on the East Coast and has also been identified as an area of exceptionally high habitat connectivity and climate change resilience.

outdoors.org • seethedark.org • darksky.org

About the Contributors

Timothy Mudie is Senior Books Editor for AMC Books. He is also an author of science fiction and fantasy whose stories have appeared on the podcast *LeVar Burton Reads* and in the magazines *Lightspeed*, *Beneath Ceaseless Skies*, and elsewhere. He lives outside Boston with his wife and two young sons.

Jenny Ward is the AMC Director of Brand Experience and has a boundless imagination with a talent for envisioning projects and guiding them to fruition. She led the Appalachian Mountain Club's effort to become the first International Dark Sky Park in New England. She lives on the shores of Moosehead Lake in Maine and finds inspiration and fortitude in the star-filled dark skies she writes about and advocates for.

Born in Maine blueberry country, Mattie Rose Templeton has been creating art since before she could speak words. Her work is inspired by the wild. Art, since the beginning, has been a way to tell stories. Mattie's goal in creating art is to take the viewer to that story-telling place. She creates using an old-fashioned inkwell and watercolor. Her work often incorporates organic geometric shapes, in a style that is uniquely her own.

About AMC

The mission of the Appalachian Mountain Club is to foster the protection, enjoyment, and understanding of the outdoors.

Since 1876 we have been working to protect the mountains, forests, waters, and trails you love in the Northeast and Mid-Atlantic regions. We envision a world where our natural resources are healthy, loved, and always protected, and where the outdoors occupies a place of central importance in every person's life. We encourage you to experience, learn more, and appreciate the outdoors knowing that your participation supports the conservation and stewardship of the natural world around you.

Join us at outdoors.org/join

Support for *If You Can See The Dark* was provided by the Maine Outdoor Heritage Fund. AMC also extends special thanks to L.L. Bean and the William T. Morris Foundation for supporting our Dark Sky education programs.

Appalachian Mountain Club is a 501(c)3 nonprofit, and sales of AMC Books fund our mission to foster the protection, enjoyment, and understanding of the outdoors. If you appreciate our efforts and would like to become a member or make a donation to AMC, visit outdoors.org, call 603-466-2727, or contact us at Appalachian Mountain Club, 10 City Square, Boston, MA 02129.

outdoors.org/books-maps

Book design by Abigail Coyle © Appalachian Mountain Club

Illustrations by Mattie Rose Templeton © Appalachian Mountain Club

Support for this project was provided by the Maine Outdoor Heritage Fund, L.L. Bean, and the William T. Morris Foundation.

ISBN 978-1-62842-187-3

The paper used in this publication meets the minimum requirements of the American National Standard for Information Sciences-Permanence of Paper for Printed Library Materials, ANSI Z39.48-1984. ∞

Interior pages are printed on responsibly harvested paper stock certified by The Forest Stewardship Council®, an independent auditor of responsible forestry practices.

Printed in Canada, using vegetable-based inks.

5 4 3 2 1   23 24 25 26 27 28